Read the book, then explore the lessons!

Becoming You!

Interactive Workbook

A Self-Discovery Tool
Companion to
Becoming Zia: A Tale of Transformation

Zia Poe Eubanks

This book is a companion to **Becoming Zia, A Tale of Transformation** available on Amazon.

Printed in the United States of America
First Printing: August 2017

ISBN: 978-0-9992133-1-5

Zia Poe Eubanks
gottacre8@gmail.com

Contents

Dedication

Becoming You! Interactive Workbook is dedicated to you, the seeker that found this book. There are no accidents in life, just interesting coincidences for soul growth. We find what we need when we're ready to learn something new.

Teachers come in all varieties. Hopefully, I can become one for you. Over the past few years I've been able to understand the drive within me that pushes me to teach and share. There is something bigger that wants to express, and I am ready to stop blocking it and let it flow. *Becoming Zia* and especially this workbook is the start of that flow.

The one thing I know for certain, we all want to be known. I mean really known, on a deeper, authentic level. That's what this work is about. First becoming known to yourself, then being that person in your everyday life, and then living a life that is aligned with your dreams, based on the truth of who you really are!

Give yourself a high five for buying this book and your willingness to do the work of Becoming You! When we are both living our truths, and following our hearts we can change the energy of the planet! Taking this step is our connection to healing. Thanks for being my partner.

If you have questions, get stuck, or just want to share anything, let me know!

Know Yourself • Be Yourself • Live It Like Crazy!

gottacre8@gmail.com

WELCOME

Thank you for reading *Becoming Zia*. I hope you enjoyed it. It was an amazing adventure while it was happening, and at times it was hard for me to get my mind around some of the experiences. I knew as soon as I came home and thought about how I was going to explain to people why I was changing my name, that I had to write the story.

It took me a while to actually get it published. I wrote the story of the trip in about 30 days. It was flowing from me. I would wake up at night with the story being told in my head. The memories, my notes, and the pictures were all there to help keep it real and the memory fresh. I got home from the Ghost Ranch in mid-September, and started writing the book on November 1st. By the end of the month the bulk of the book was complete. In December, I had surgery on my throat and then life started happening.

Here it is, nearly four years later! I was determined to get it finished. More importantly I wanted to share the story, and hopefully help other people get in touch with that place I found. The "unfucked" place. That place where I can stop trying to fix myself and start living life more fully. Today I am grateful, and feel a true sense of accomplishment that not only is the book published, but I have created this workbook as a tool for you! That makes me very happy.

I sincerely hope that this workbook will help you examine and explore some of your beliefs and begin living a life more aligned with your heart. All of us have something within us that wants to express itself; if you haven't found that for yourself, I hope this workbook nudges you in the right direction.

With gratitude and big love,

Zia

"It is better to live your own destiny imperfectly than to live an imitation of someone else's life with perfection."

- The Bhagavad Gita

INTRODUCTION

What can Becoming Zia teach you?

All the experiences and lessons that I wrote about it the book really are universal. We all have life experiences and a history to draw from, to explore and to learn. Life is our school.

Obviously, the experience of *Becoming Zia* profoundly changed me. It has taken me some time to fully embrace the changes and realize the depth of it all. I didn't realize it then, but now understand that my experience is a set of lessons that are universal. And, very basic at the core. The hard part is letting go of all the seemingly important clutter to discover the real truth of the matter.

This workbook is your guide to help you discover the real truth of your life. It is going to take some exploring, digging, and asking yourself some difficult questions. You can do it. This workbook will help you figure out your unique gifts, learn to let go of what isn't working, and embrace life in a new way! It's your guide to *Becoming You!*

Take your time to thoughtfully answer the questions and do the work suggested. I know it will benefit you in ways you can't imagine. Any time you do this type of self-discovery work, it opens you to a new level of consciousness. When you see things differently, then you do things differently.

How it works:

The workbook is separated into a set of themes that relate to anyone and everyone. Then, there are activities on each theme to help you uncover or expose areas in your life or beliefs that are holding you back. The themes are correlated with *Becoming Zia*, and explore many of the same topics.

The themes follow a pattern. The first section theme is **Know Yourself**. In this section, you will explore your life from a new angle and possibly uncover some buried dreams or recognize a pattern that is keeping you stuck. Getting to really know yourself is key before you can really become you! Most of us are holding on to some role or personality trait that was put on us earlier in our lives. And let me tell you, it's time to let that stuff (shit) go!

The second theme is **Be Yourself**. In this section, you will explore your gifts, get real about the truth of who you are, and claim your wholeness. It seems that the word "authentic self" has been thrown around so much that it's just another catch phrase. But the truth is, it's a very real thing that you need to explore and understand. We are all great at downplaying our gifts and focusing on our flaws. When you really uncover your true self, then it's a no brainer to celebrate and own the reality of the authentic you! It's powerful and liberating!

And the final theme is **Live It Like Crazy!** Once you know yourself and become yourself, you can make a plan for the life you want to live, follow your dreams, and begin taking action in a big way to make it happen. That is *Becoming You!* It's time to let the past go, own your gifts, and follow your passion with no excuses!

Know Yourself

Be Yourself

Live It Like Crazy!

Does that sound like a lot to get from this workbook? It is! I am hoping that reading Becoming Zia started you thinking, which will make answering the questions and completing the workbook much easier.

However, before you start working on the themes there is pre-theme work to do! That is a review of the "big lessons" from the book. We are going to start from the end, and then move forward.

So, let's get started. I can't wait for you to uncover the secrets of you and start living life full on! It's time!

The BIG Lessons

Once I finished writing *Becoming Zia* and some time passed, I could see more clearly the bigger lessons I discovered during my journey. This is the key to beginning to open up and explore the themes in this workbook, which are about you and your life. If you are stuck in some of these lessons, it is going to be harder to make it through to the **Live It Like Crazy** phase! And, I want that for all of you. In countdown style, I'll start with lesson number four.

Lesson 4: What other people think of you is none of your business

This is a big one! I spent most of my life outwardly focused. I was either feeling judged, or judging other people. It wasn't until I really got this lesson that my life changed. What really brought it home for me is when I finally let it sink into my thick skull that I had absolutely NO control over other people, what they thought, or their opinion of me. It was impossible for me to really know what they were thinking, and if I made it up in my head, which is what I did, it was all just a big story that I concocted and lived out as my reality – none of which was true or could be proven in any way. I just spun my wheels in frustration, became distracted from myself, and stayed in a perpetual state of not feeling good enough.

Do you know how liberating it is to let go of what other people are thinking? It is crazy liberating! And, it is the only sensible thing to do. When you begin to understand that what other people are thinking is none of your business you can start to see other big truths, like you are not responsible for other people's feelings! Wow! It's true. But, I'll stay on this topic for now.

5

Let's begin to explore this lesson. Throughout this workbook, I'll be asking questions and giving you space to answer. This book is made to write in. To scribble, draw, doodle, print, write cursive, whatever – just get ideas and thoughts out of your head and on the paper! Go buy some colored markers or a new fountain pen! Be vulnerable and honest, and question yourself. Don't put your guard up; forget that! Let it rip, open up, and explore and investigate anything that feels like it needs to be exposed to the light! Go for it!

Are you ready? Here we go!

What is the first thing that pops in your head (write it down) when you hear the phrase "What other people think of me is none of my business."

What do you want to think?

How far apart are the two thoughts?

What would it take for you to fully own the thought you want to think?

How would your life be different if you held that thought as your reality?

Who would be affected by you having that new thought?

How would your life be different? Would you be doing something different, or living someplace different, or have a new job?

Honestly, how much power do other people have over your decisions? What would it take for you to fully own this lesson?

Lesson 3: We are in total control of our own happiness!

When I learned this lesson, it pissed me off. I had lived in the victim mentality for so long, blaming other people and situations for my unhappiness, that when I discovered that I had all the responsibility for my happiness, I really was mad. All this time I had the power and I was giving it away.

Everything that is happening is happening as a thought before it becomes a reality. And the only place thoughts come from in my life, are from my mind. I had become so used to the knee jerk thought pattern of "poor me." I was abused as a kid, I *was* molested, I was a battered wife, I never had a chance, blah, blah, blah. It never occurred to me that I had free choice over my thoughts.

I'd been studying *new thought* for years. I've read a dozen books on the Law of Attraction, and I thought I understood the concepts well. I even belong to a spiritual community whose basic principles are about the science of the mind, yet I didn't fully get it until after this experience of *Becoming Zia*. We are the creator. Everything we think is creation. We are creating our lives every moment. When I realized that, I realized that no one could take my happiness away. I had to let them. I had all the power. So, if I had the power to give it away, I had the power to take it back! And I did. I am in control of my own happiness. Simple as that!

Is it that simple? Do you recognize you are in control of your own happiness?

Who have you given your happiness power to? Why?

Are you happy with that? Do they make you
happy? Is it possible? If not, why?

If believing that you are the creator of your life, by your
thoughts, what are you creating in your life?

What would change if you took full responsibility for your own happiness?

How different would your life be if you were actually
in charge of your own happiness?

©Zia Poe Eubanks

Lesson 2: Setting boundaries is about you, not the other person!

There have been a lot of "light bulb" moments in my life, but this is one of the greatest and most healing for me. I never learned how to set boundaries. They didn't exist in my world in any sort of healthy way as a child. As an adult, when I thought of a boundary I always thought it was setting a hardline with someone and being firm. It was sticking up for myself in a way that put the other person in their place, and that was something I had no ability to do without being a total bitch or in a rage. I had no healthy boundary setting ability or knowledge, but I desperately needed to learn this.

Then, miraculously one day I got it – thanks to Brooke Castillo from The Life Coach School. I was listening to one of her podcasts and the message slammed me. I realized that I was holding onto resentment like a badge of honor. There were people in my life who had "wronged" me in my mind, and I could not let go of the resentment! I felt that if I let go of the resentment it would let them off the hook for their bad behavior. That day, I realized that it was my inability to set a boundary and allowing people to treat me in a way I should not have tolerated that was the real issue. My resentment towards them was just a smoke screen that kept me safe in my victimhood. If I had set a boundary, and had limits to what kind of behavior or situations I would allow myself to be subjected to, then I would not have any resentment at all. I would have set a boundary and moved on with my life, fully empowered. It had nothing to do with the other person! (Picture a giant light bulb turning on here!)

When I recognized that, all the resentment I was holding floated away. Then I had to take full responsibility for my life, my decisions and the results it had created. Hard as hell, but really amazing healing!

How are you at setting boundaries?

Are you holding resentment towards someone or some situation?

Can you see your role in that situation? What could you do differently?

If you could set a boundary now, what would it be and for what reason?

How would setting that boundary change your life?

Do you see how setting boundaries is about you, and not the other person? How does that feel?

How would your life be different? Would you be doing something different, or living someplace different, or have a new job?

Honestly, how much power do other people have over your decisions? What would it take for you to fully own this lesson?

Lesson 1: You and your life are perfect just as they are!

This is the lesson I call the "unfuck yourself" paradigm shift. I lived most of my life trying to recover from being "fucked up." I had a crappy childhood, an abusive marriage, a drug and alcohol addiction, lousy cars, low paying jobs, crappy self-esteem. Poor me. More victim mentality and therapy, and self-help books and more therapy, etcetera, etcetera. It was more of Lesson 3. I was creating my own reality. I believed I was a fucked up mess, and I was. As time went on and I did get better, then I was a survivor! I was still a mess, but I was a better mess. I had survived all that shit and I was proud of myself! Yay me!

Then one day I realized that victim and survivor are just two ends of the same dysfunction. Sure, being a survivor is better, but it is still defining your life by the abuse or trauma. When I could let go of identifying with either of them, I knew I was headed in the right direction.

I am on a journey, and I have always been. It's the same journey you are on. We all are. It's the journey to wholeness. A spiritual teacher I once had told me it's a journey to remembering. Remembering our own perfection. Years ago, I heard that, and I believed him, but I never really understood it until after the Ghost Ranch. Then I got it.

My life is perfect. So is yours. I am perfect. I am having the exact experiences I need to have for the growth of my soul. It is my journey of making my way back to the truth. The truth of who I really am. A part of the divine. A wave in the ocean. It's true! You are that too!

This life, your life, is the perfect match for you. You made exactly the right decisions so you could learn what you needed to learn to bring you back to remembering.

Okay. I may be losing some of you here. That may seem like too big of a pill to swallow. I get it. I get how there are decisions in life you wish you hadn't made, and things that look like mistakes or even tragedies. But, just stay with me and imagine it is true. Imagine that every single thing that ever happened to you is neutral and happened *for* you so you could learn, grow, or just see things differently. If you don't judge it, and just see it as your perfect life, how would that change things?

Have you ever considered yourself "fucked up"?

If you answered yes, write about what that means to you.

If you answered no, then write about why you feel that way. (Congrats, by the way!)

*Is there some reason you don't want to accept things
that have happened to you in your life as perfect?*

Are you holding onto judgment? What is that about?

Are you holding onto shame, regret, sadness? Explain.

*If you could let go of all that and accept that everything that
happened was exactly what you needed, how would it feel?*

How would your life be different if you did?

How would you be different if you accepted yourself unconditionally?

Can you accept that you're perfect exactly as you are, no changes needed?

How do you feel about the concept that life is a set of lessons leading you back to discovering your own connection to perfection?

More space for answers

Section 1:
KNOW YOURSELF

"Knowing yourself is the beginning of all wisdom."

— *Aristotle*

The first theme is **Know Yourself**. It is the first step in *Becoming You*. It makes no sense to start anywhere else. Until you know yourself, it is impossible to begin living the big life you richly deserve!

When I started my journey to New Mexico, I promised myself that I would be open to everything and not hold back. I approached it as an opportunity to change my life, and I was willing to not stop myself out of fear, embarrassment, or "looking stupid." I tried to set aside all the things that normally stop me from making the changes I needed in my life. That's what I am asking you to do here. Approach this work with an open mind. Put down your defenses and be vulnerable. Drop the armor and really look at yourself and be gentle. This is discovery work. You are excavating your life. There is treasure to be found!

Dreams

Going to the Painting from the Wild Heart Retreat at the Ghost Ranch in New Mexico was a dream I had for 10 years. What I realized was it turned into a fantasy, not a dream. I fantasized about being able to escape to New Mexico and take time just for me to explore my creativity. It was a fantasy I used to escape from my life. I'm not sure I ever believed it would happen. It wasn't until I was in a mastermind group and they challenged me to go for it that I actually believed it could happen. Thankfully, I had that wonderful mastermind group! Otherwise, it would have been an unfulfilled fantasy.

Do you have some dream/fantasy in your life? Something you have in your head that stays in your head?

How big is it? Life changing? Why would it change your life?

Or, is it something small and nagging? How would you feel if you finally did it?

Have you given up dreaming altogether? If so, how come? What is going on in your life that has taken away your ability to dream?

What has answering these questions brought up for you?

Illness and Body Issues

My first big insight into knowing myself was the discovery of the tumor in my throat. It became the focus of healing and also the uncovering of a lifetime of issues. I had been feeling plagued with thyroid issues for years; my focus was healing my dis-ease. Then I was diagnosed with a tumor on my parathyroid, which has nothing to do with the thyroid – it's just thyroid adjacent in the body. It was like the Universe was trying to tell me to pay attention and when the thyroid wasn't enough, it added the tumor. Like a brick hitting me in the head, I had to pay attention. The light finally came on, and I realized all these throat issues had a bigger meaning!

To really know yourself, you have to be in touch with your body too. Is your body trying to tell you something you are ignoring? You'll know when you review your life and can see a trend in an illness or a recurring body theme. Do you have backaches or constant bronchitis? Do you have foot problems or stress headaches? Think about your life, stress, aches, pains, and illness. Is there a theme? My throat that was the center of my issues; when I finally started paying attention the healing finally began. The healing was about my life, but manifested in my throat.

Below is a chart showing the chakra energy centers and the body parts and organs associated with each one. Review this for a few minutes, then answer the questions.

There is tons of information on the internet about the chakras. You can find anything you want to learn about identifying issues related to each chakra and all sorts of healing modalities. There are also lots of good books. Not only on chakras, but on emotional manifestation of illness. Caroline Myss and Louise L. Hay are pioneers in the field. Both are very good resources.

I found a Reiki practitioner who was very helpful and really did work wonders for balancing my energy. There are so many resources. Take your time and investigate your unique body–spirit connection and see what you can uncover!

Chakra
Energy Centers

sahasrara - crown chakra
thousandfold

ajna - third eye chakra
awareness

vishuddha - throat chakra
purity

anahata - heart chakra
flawless

manipura - solar plexus chakra
sparkling/jewel

svadhisthana - sacral chakra
sweetness

muladhara - root chakra
support

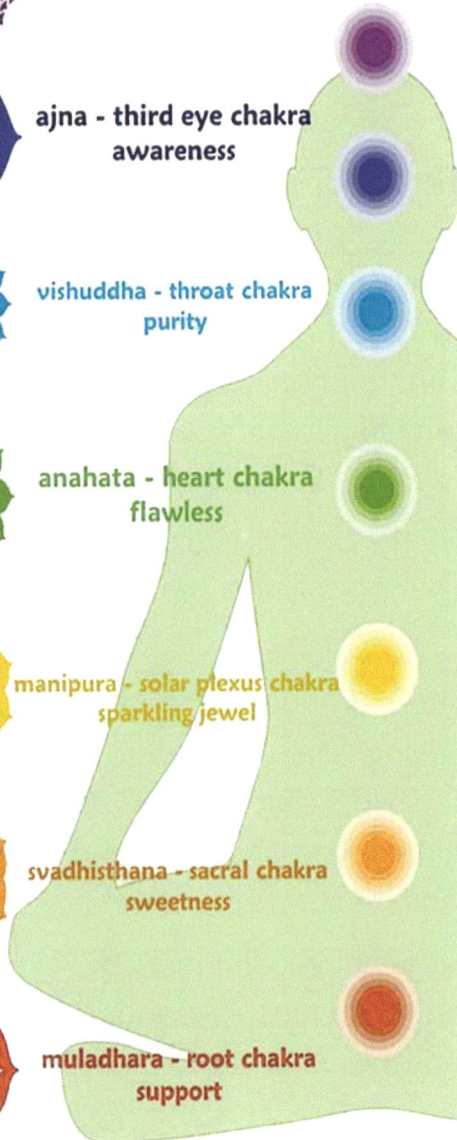

7th Crown: Pineal gland; regulates biological cycles, including sleep. Spinal cord, brain, migraine, immune system, dementia, learning difficulties, depression.

6th Third Eye: Pituitary gland, eyes, brain, headaches, high blood pressure, insomnia, sinus, scalp, nervous disorders.

5th Throat: Thyroid gland; regulates body temperature and metabolism. Bronchial tubes, vocal cords, respiratory system, all areas of the mouth, upper arms, tonsils.

4th Heart: Thymus gland; regulates the immune system. Heart, lungs, breasts, congestion, bronchitis, circulation problems.

3rd Solar Plexus: Intestines, pancreas, liver, bladder, stomach, upper spine, kidneys, ulcers, heartburn, gallstones, food allergies.

2nd Sacral: Adrenal glands; regulates the immune system. Bladder, prostate, ovaries, kidneys, gallbladder, bowel, spleen, back, hips, menstruation, cystitis, overeating.

1st Root: Reproductive glands, sex organs, addictive behaviors, ankles, feet, knees, spine, skin problems.

After reviewing the chart, what area of your body
do you think is your problem area?

How long have you had issues in that area?

Can you identify a time period or incident that first made you aware of it?

What do you think this physical issue is **really** about?

If you are not sure, then write an educated guess
based on the evidence you have gathered.

©Zia Poe Eubanks

What is the message your body is trying to give you?

Healing Map

During the Painting from the Wild Heart Retreat, I painted a healing map of my throat. The physical depiction of what all my throat issues represented helped me begin the process of changing my life and healing my throat. Here is a picture of my healing map. I wrote words on my head and mouth – Smile, Stuff, Intellectualize, and Deny. These were the methods I used to ignore my feelings and not speak my truth. By doing that, I held down Fear, Wants, Value, Voice, Truth, Desires, and Anger. In the middle was my throat, my thyroid, my parathyroid, and the tumor. It all became very clear.

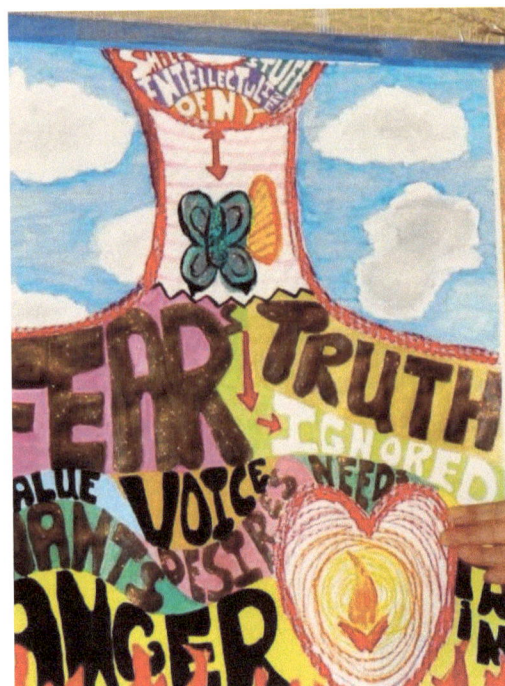

Now, I want you to think about what your map would look like. Think about the part of your body and what messages are trying to come through. Use the next page to draw, design, or write about your own personal healing map.

It doesn't have to look like mine. Use your imagination and design what your map would represent for you. You could even make a collage with pictures and words from magazines, or your own family photographs. Treat it like a scrapbook page, and tell the story of your body and the messages it is trying to tell you.

This is an important assignment. When your body is holding emotional blockages, it is primed for dis-ease and illness. If you want to learn more about this, Dr. Lissa Rankin has written a book called *Mind Over Medicine*. It is a real eye-opener!

On the next page, I want you to create your map. Take your time and let your creativity flow!

Healing Map

Road Blocks and Other Distractions

It is interesting how we can set up road blocks and distractions in order to avoid connecting with ourselves. It is much easier to disappoint yourself or give up on your dreams than let other people down (or our self-perceived responsibilities). Or, you can be like me; I tried to people please my way to love and acceptance. It didn't work at all, and I ended up exhausted, stressed out, and resentful! What people pleasing did for me was keep me distracted. So did my shame and regrets, irrational fears, anxiety, and my obsession with my body and weight. Not to mention the time I spent trying to find the latest natural remedy for healing my thyroid disease, which became a part-time job. Nevertheless, they were all distractions. Real, yes. Some seemed really important, yet they were still distractions.

The hard part is getting honest, and separating the seemingly important from the need to use it as a distraction. Let me give you some examples. As long as I was focusing all my attention on losing weight and hating my body, I didn't have to think about my unhappy marriage. When I started thinking about some past regret or shameful event, I could cringe and feel like a victim and I didn't have to take responsibility for my life. When I didn't set boundaries or stick up for myself and my values, I could feel like a martyr, sacrificing myself for someone or some situation, instead of standing in my strength and integrity. This is the stuff that keeps us from being known to others and to ourselves. As long as we are willing to stuff our feelings, ignore our values, and put other people's needs ahead of our own, then being known will never happen.

Is this something you want? Is it something you are willing to uncover? Because you can't go on to the next step **Be Yourself** until you are honestly willing to look at yourself and know yourself at a true, honest, face value, no masks or disguises level. Didn't I tell you this was going to be hard? (But really worth it!)

Below is a list of possible distractors. Review the list and circle the ones that you feel might be something you do. Even if it is only occasionally, circle it. Take your time and give this some thought.

Distractors

Mark all that apply

Regrets	Over Committing
Shame	Escaping into Books
Fears- Rational & Irrational	Netflix, Hulu, TV
Weight/Body Obsession	Eating/Binging
Jealousy	Sick Days/Missing Work
Drinking/Drugs	Depression
Shopping	Exercise/Working Out
People Pleasing	Victimhood
Over Achieving	Childhood History
Under Achieving	Internet, technology
Escape into Work or Kids	Art/Crafts/Creativity
Helping Other People	Craft/Art Supplies Addiction
Super Volunteer	Blaming other people or person

Other (list below)

Were you honest? Good for you! This workbook is for your eyes only. Feel free to be brutally honest, and don't worry about sharing any of this. This is your discovery tool. Congrats on doing this work. When you are really honest, it's hard not to see that it is so easy to get caught up in distractors. It is built into our culture. Don't blame yourself. Just become aware that these distractions are keeping you for being known to others and most importantly yourself. It is time to change that.

What did you discover? Write down three or four of your top distractors.

What do you think these distractors are keeping well hidden?

Was that hard for you to write? Why?

What would happen if you stopped using the distractors?

Who are you without them?

Who do you want to be?

How would your life look if you gave them up?

After doing this work, what are your thoughts on who you are and being known (to yourself)?

Who are you and what do you want?

What does the real you, from the inside, want to express?

Below, I want you to write a description of yourself that you can read later that proves you have a real sense of yourself. Describe yourself in detail. Write about your dreams. Explain what you feel is inside of you that wants to be expressed! If you need more room, get a notebook or some blank sheets of paper?

Section 2:
BE YOURSELF

*"Don't change so people will like you. Be yourself
and the right people will love you!"*

— *Author unknown*

*"If you can just be yourself, then you have to be
original because there's no one like you."*

— *Marc Newson*

Just be yourself! That is something I had been trying to be for years. Except I never thought that was enough. I always had to do more, be more, do it perfectly, and that still was not enough. That's because I hadn't fully learned **Lesson 4: What Other People Think of You is None of Your Business**.

What I did know is that I had some gifts. I was especially clear that I was creative, organized, a good teacher, and I could figure out almost anything. I accepted that and would timidly own those traits. I had a sense of who I was and that I had some gifts, but that nagging "fucked-up-ness" still hung over me like a dark cloud.

At the Ghost Ranch, that cloud started to lift when I painted my first painting. It started off seeming pretty silly, big round circles painted in blues and greens. But it ended up helping me process the separation I had created from my innate gifts, and I was able to embrace and own them again. It was pretty miraculous. It was the theme for the trip really – letting go of all the blocks standing in the way of seeing myself whole and owning the abilities that made me the unique human being I am. When I painted the last circle red, representing my heart, and then connected all the circles with "veins" with blood running through them – making them a system again – I felt it. It was like being awakened and deciding to just own it – accept the gifts, internalize them, and be whole. It was pretty awesome. Here is the painting – it is no masterpiece – but it was a process I went through that was all about symbolism and color.

The truth of the matter, I always knew who I was and what my gifts were. What I couldn't do was allow myself to believe they mattered. It was like I believed that if I was good at something, then it must not be that big a deal. That's because I had a screen of distractors blocking me.

Now that we have been exploring your distractors and have some awareness of what has been keeping you blocked and "unknown" to yourself, it's time to explore your gifts!

Owning Your Gifts

You know. It's usually not a secret. We all have a sense of ourselves and what makes us feel alive. My granddaughter Bella has a girlfriend who is totally into bugs and insects. Whenever she is with us, she is our walking, talking, Wikipedia search for any encounter with a bug. It's interesting to watch this very timid girl suddenly start talking about bugs with a passion that lights her up! It just makes me smile and look for more bugs to talk about! Because that's the other thing. When someone is connected to their "thing" and their excitement is apparent, it is contagious and magnetic! Seeing that in someone else reminds us of that feeling. This is being authentic. It's so real.

What is something that makes your heart beat
faster and makes you begin to feel excited?

Is there something you do that everyone knows you for?

*In your head, you know the things you find easy
to do and enjoyable. Write them down.*

*How do you feel when someone says, "That's my
life purpose, I was born to do this!"*

There are many things that make you unique. What are they?

*If you had to describe your life purpose, what would it be? Does your
life fit that description? If not, why? If yes, how do you create it?*

Two Yous

There are two yous, admit it. Imagine going out to lunch with your best friend. How do you behave? What's your comfort level? How honest and real are you? Think about that.

Then imagine meeting some business associates for lunch. You have a concept you want to share, and it could mean a promotion. How do you behave?

When I was at the Ranch, I remember one of the women talking about "playing roles." She said she had spent her life playing the role she thought she was expected to play. This wasn't based on her true self, but on what she imagined other people wanted her to be. When she said that, I really understood. I felt the same way. I wondered what it would be like to just be myself all the time.

Here's the thing – the more time you spend connected to what feels the most real to you, the happier you'll be! The key is to understand yourself, know yourself, and start being yourself. The next exercise will help you look at yourself more clearly.

First, write your name in the center of the form.

On the inner ring of blue ovals, write the words that describe the you that you present to the world. Or you could put what roles you play. You decide what would help you the most. The important thing is to write about the you that you show the world.

Then on the outside ring of yellow circles, write words or phrases that represent the you that you feel inside – your bigger self, who you really are and want to be.

Looking at the contrast of these two should give you some insight into who you are and who you want to be. This is similar to the circles I painted at the ranch. This is an opportunity to open up and look at the parts of yourself you want to own and the ones you want (or may need) to let go.

Take your time with this exercise. Give it careful thought, and be honest with yourself.

Two Yous

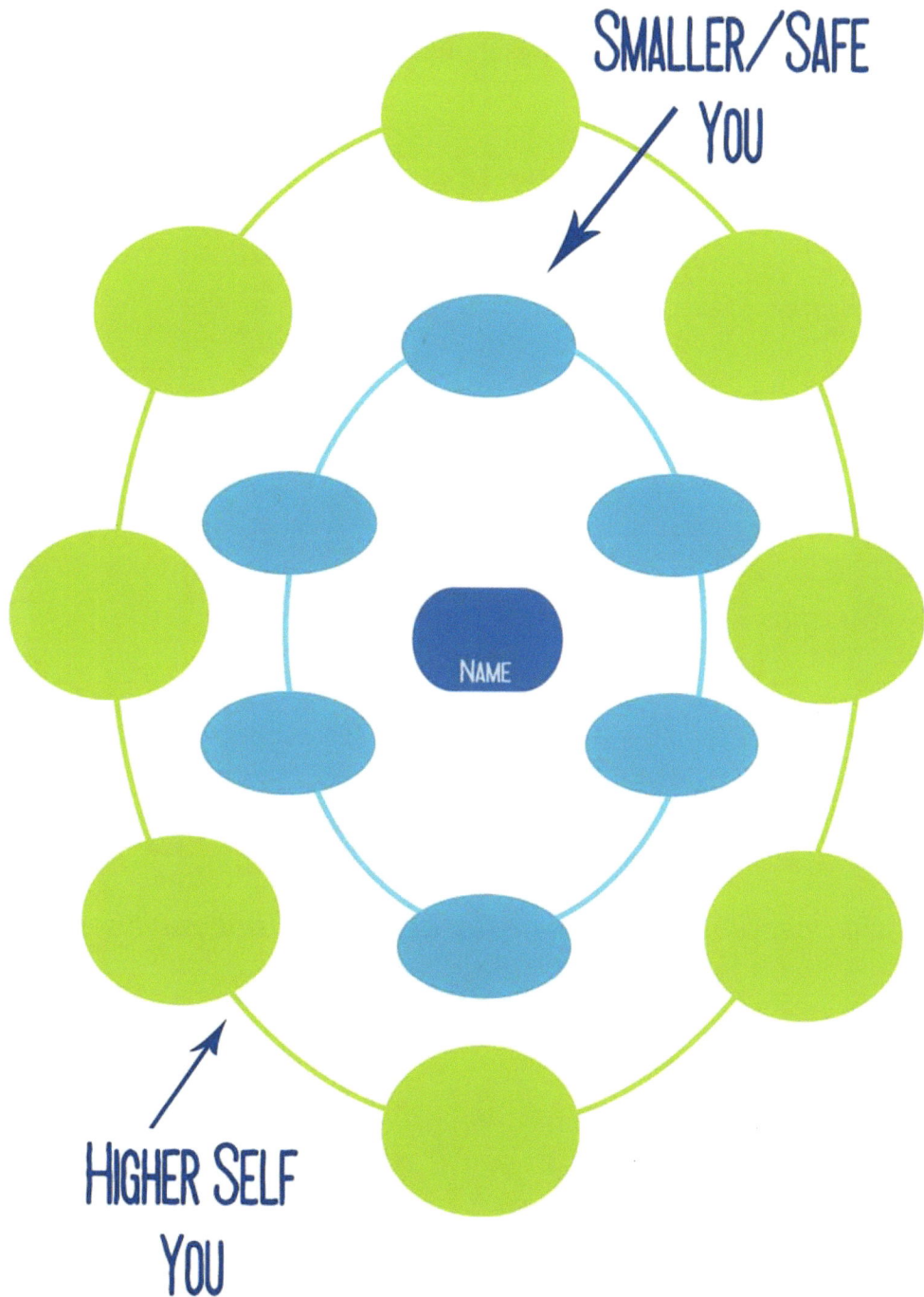

SMALLER/SAFE YOU

Name

HIGHER SELF YOU

The Truth of You

What is the truth of you? What I found out about myself is that I am creative, passionate, adventurous, and I have a need to be known and know people on a deep level. I enjoy people, but also love quiet time to be still and write. There is something in me that wants to express itself. Writing my book and this workbook are part of that expression.

What is the truth of you? You know what it is! Take your time, dive in, and answer as honestly as you can

Write a description of yourself.

What are your gifts? List them.

What do other people see in you, or say about you that you know is true?

What is your greatest accomplishment?

Or is your greatest accomplishment yet to be? What is it?

Claiming Your Wholeness

All it takes to claim your wholeness is to just do it. It doesn't require acknowledgement from anyone, just you. The state of being whole is a thought. A belief. Is it possible for you to believe that you are whole and complete exactly as you are at this minute?

It was a hard concept for me to get at first. But as I thought about it, I realized that the only person who could judge that was me. I had to accept my wholeness and be at peace. It was that simple.

Sure, the events of the two weeks in New Mexico helped me along in that process big time, but it is possible any time. All it requires is recognizing who you are and accepting that completely – unconditional self-acceptance. That's mind-boggling, right? something that seems impossible?

I'm not saying you just throw in the towel and just lie on the couch and watch Netflix and eat Dove candies. (Well, if that's what you want to do, go for it.) I'm saying, there is nothing to fix, you are who you are, and it's time to own your gifts and get on with your life. Playing small is not serving anyone!

The Marianne Williamson quote that so many people quote is so right on, and appropriate here. So, I'm going to use it!

"Our deepest fear is not that we are inadequate. Our deepest fear is that we are powerful beyond measure. It is our light, not our darkness, that most frightens us. You're playing small does not serve the world."

— *Marianne Williamson*

©Zia Poe Eubanks

When you read that quote, what are your first thoughts?

What is blocking you from accepting your wholeness?

What would it take for you to claim it?

What if it were a fake it until you make it situation? How could you "act as if" you were whole? What would that look like?

Imagine creating a wholeness ritual, claiming your wholeness. What could you do to symbolically claim it? Create one! Write your ideas here.

Section 3:
LIVE IT LIKE CRAZY

The goal of this workbook is to help you process some of the lessons from *Becoming Zia* in your own life. The biggest one for me is the recognition that I was living my life for other people nearly all of my life.

When I had the memory of my mom calling me her "living doll," it opened my mind. She told me she had seen a cute little girl on a television show one night, and her name was Cindy. That is how I got my name. Before I was born, she worked in a doll factory and she also talked about how she loved the doll clothes. So, when I was born, she loved dressing me up. I was literally her "living doll." Isn't that crazy?

So, my connection to myself and my name was based on my mother's fantasy. My name never fit me, and I wasn't a living doll. I was born a unique, one-of-a-kind human being. No matter how much she tried to mold me, it never worked. When the name Zia came to me, I knew it was meant to be. It was an acknowledgement of my process, the process of really knowing myself for the first time in my life

Fitting In Your Own Skin

Along with this realization came a sense of fitting in my own skin for the first time as well. That is a big deal. Just walking around feeling connected in mind and body is huge. Losing touch or living based on your guess of what other people want you to be is so fragmenting. It is destructive on every level! The freedom and joy of being connected and feeling comfortable in your own skin is a fantastic feeling!

Does your name fit you? Have you ever thought about changing it?

©Zia Poe Eubanks

Who do you want to be known as?

Do you feel comfortable in your own skin?

What would it take to make that a possibility?

Are there people in your life who would object to you changing?

What is holding you back from it?

What are you willing to do to begin living your life as you?

What would "Living It Like Crazy" look like in your life?

The Freedom of Simplicity

When it became clear that we had to downsize in order for my husband to function at his best, it was hard. But, I had been fantasizing about living small for a long time. The simplicity of it seemed so appealing. So when I had to do it in real life, I was excited and honestly looking forward to getting rid of a lot of junk we never used. It was a process. But in the end, it was amazing and so freeing! That's when I realized how stuff is like all the emotional clutter we covered in the other sections. It's just junk holding you back from being real. It's the physical manifestation of "baggage." Letting it go is cathartic and healing! I am happier living small than I ever have been in my life. It is awesome.

Are you holding onto a lot of clutter?

What does it represent for you?

Can you see the connection between emotional baggage and physical clutter?

Do you have a lot of stuff because it makes you feel like you matter or you're deserving?

Do you have a shopping distraction (addiction)?

When you think of downsizing, how does it make you feel?

What is standing in the way of you living more simply?

When you think of living your best life, how does this topic fit into that?

Describe in detail how you want your environment?

Crazy Dreams

Most of my life I wanted to write. I blogged, did "Morning Pages" for years, wrote poetry, and started about 10 different books. It was something I loved, but never fully followed through with. I even started a subscription newsletter in the 90's called "The Joy Path." Writing was a dream.

Guess what? I just published my first book *Becoming Zia*! And, this is my second! That is a crazy dream! A crazy dream that came true! What changed?

First, I stopped living for other people and started living for myself. Secondly, and more importantly, I connected with the real me. And I approved of her! I support her and encourage her. I am her biggest fan! That feels good to write and even better to feel!

The key to "Living It Like Crazy!" is doing the work of knowing yourself and being you, and then living your dreams!

What are your dreams?

What do you want to be doing? Where do you want to be living?

What do you want to be doing that you're not?

Or, do you not know what you want? Have you given up dreaming?

What's stopping you?

Take a few minutes to yourself, find a relaxing quiet spot, and just take some time to imagine a life that excites you. It can be totally imaginary; just do it. Let it rip. Just practice dreaming. Lying on a beach in the Bahamas, reading a book on the deck of a mountain cottage, being the CEO of your own company, volunteering to build schools in Africa, anything! Write your fantasy/dream below.

©Zia Poe Eubanks

More space for exploring your dreams:

BECOMING YOU!

"When you know yourself you are empowered. When you accept yourself you are invincible!"

— Tina Lifford

"The privilege of a lifetime is being who you are."

— Joseph Campbell

Here we are. At the end of the workbook. The place where you get to claim the real you and start thinking about the rest of your life! Exciting and scary! Hopefully, this workbook has helped you identify some truths about you, and given you an idea of where you want to head in the future.

On the next page, there is the **Becoming You Proclamation**. It is for you to fill out and do with whatever you choose. I hope you hang it on the wall, or make it part of a vision board!

When you think about the three parts of this workbook, **Know Yourself**, **Be Yourself**, and **Live It Like Crazy**, you'll know which area needs your attention. That is what this discovery book is all about. Don't let that stop you from filling out your proclamation! You know who you really are and what you really want, even if you think you don't. It's there. You just have to trust it, and ignore the fear of what you think it would require to live it.

When I came back from the Ghost Ranch to my real life, it was shocking. I had changed so much, and everyone else was the same. They expected me to be the same. But, I wasn't and I couldn't be. That disappointed some people, and thrilled others. But as I learned in Lesson 4, *what other people think of me is none of my business*. So, I knew I had to be myself, honor myself, and do what had to be done, no matter what happened. I was determined.

It turned out perfect! Not entirely as I expected, but perfect. You know why? Because when I learned to really know myself, accept myself unconditionally, and live based on my true feelings, not what others expected or wanted, I was at peace. Then I could accept whatever life had to bring my way. And I could do it with a smile on my face!

I love my life. I live in a beautiful place, in our tiny house. Life is simple and adventurous. I have a lovely cottage for my meditation/spiritual practice and for being creative. I have freedom, abundance, and time to do exactly what I want. I have wonderful family and friends. Life is good!

That's what I am hoping you can begin to find from doing this workbook. It's there, within. It always has been. Just waiting. Waiting for the time when you were ready to truly step into your authentic power. I know this sounds like buzz words, but they are true. It's why we're all here — to have this human experience, which includes good and bad, happiness and tragedy, laughter and tears. It's being human. But, what happens, we get so wrapped up in the lessons of being human that we forget we are really spiritual beings first, experiencing being human. When you remember that, it changes everything in a big way.

Living from that space of connecting with your higher self, and stepping back and being a witness to your human experience instead of getting all wrapped up in the drama is what needs to happen. The more you connect with that truth the easier and easier it will be to step back. When life comes at you and you can just smile, chuckle, and think to yourself "being human is a trip!" Just let all the judgement go — you're there. I hope that for all of you!

> *"We are not human beings in search of a spiritual experience.*
> *We are spiritual beings immersed in a human experience."*
>
> — *Wayne Dyer*

Becoming You! Proclamation
Know Yourself ♥ Be Yourself ♥ Live It Like Crazy!

_____

Name

Whereas, from this day forward _____

will be known as _____ .

The following words describe her/him:

_____, _____, _____,

_____, _____, _____,

_____, and _____.

Whereas, _____, willingly and

enthusiastically accepts his/her following gifts:

_____, _____, _____,

_____, _____, _____,

_____, and wholly owns them.

Whereas, the signing of the document, _____

will honor life fully, _____

commits to living it like crazy!

_____   _____

Signature   *Date*

"Knowing yourself is the
beginning of all wisdom.."

- Aristotle

WHERE TO GO FROM HERE

"Create a life that feels good on the inside, not one that just looks good on the outside."

— *Author unknown*

Great job! You did some hard work. I'm excited to hear about how you decided to live your life like crazy! Please feel free to email me or connect with me on Facebook and let me know what you're up to!

My *Becoming Zia* experience changed me forever. What I am learning more and more about every day is my purpose. I've felt the need to express myself since I came home from New Mexico. Writing the book was the beginning. Now, I realize that the biggest thing within wanting to express is the idea of being known, knowing people, and connecting to the "realness." My doing that is what initiated this workbook and my new website. It will continue the work of the lessons I learned. It boils down to the tagline I created: **Know Yourself**, **Be Yourself**, and **Live It Like Crazy**. By doing that, the energy of my life and your life is going to elevate the energy wherever we are. And that is a really good thing!

It is starting with my website, www.ZiaPoe.com. I will be writing weekly articles about the lessons and the three concepts. You can get the weekly updates via email by signing up on my website, or by following me on my Facebook page: www.facebook.com/BecomingZia.

In 2018, I plan to introduce a workshop series and e-books that will teach more about these lessons and concepts. So, look for more information about that in the months to come.

My best to you on your adventure and the journey to *Becoming You*!

In the spirit of being known,

Zia

Special Note About ANXIETY

I have suffered from anxiety most of my life, but I didn't know it. I adapted to it and made corrective behaviors- some good, some not so good. I knew I had issues with tight spaces, being in social situations, and I was always so uncomfortable when there was too much attention focused on me.

It wasn't until I wrote *Becoming Zia* and was editing the book that I began to see how anxiety was such a big part of my life. Then after a very stressful couple of years, my body finally broke down and said "enough." I was rushed to the hospital, thinking I was having a heart attack or stroke, but it was a major anxiety attack and emotional breakdown.

I have never felt so scared or vulnerable. Thank goodness, my daughter came to my rescue and helped me get back on my feet. I had to go back into therapy, see a psychiatrist, and was put on medication. I had been against meds for a long time, but I knew I needed them. I absolutely could not control my body, and the panic and anxiety attacks were debilitating! I understand now what people meant when they talked about having an emotional breakdown. It is so frightening.

You've read about my anxiety issues in *Becoming Zia*, but I wanted to bring it up here again. It is something real and also treatable. There seems to be so much stigma attached to mental illness. I get it, because I was that way. Both my parents had mental illness and I could barely acknowledge that at the beginning, much less acknowledge it in myself. Now I get it. Mental illness is illness in your brain. Mine stemmed from my childhood. Traumatic events I was too young to deal with caused me to suffer post-traumatic stress disorder (PTSD), which progressed as I got older and manifested into a full-blown anxiety disorder.

Thankfully, I am okay now. I received treatment and still take medicine for anxiety. I learned some very important tools to use when I feel anxious. One of the big ones is not identifying with the anxiety. When I realized that the anxiety was happening to me, but it was NOT me, it gave me a sense of control. THAT is powerful, especially with anxiety. I also started practicing Transcendental Meditation, which helped immensely. I highly recommend it!

If you feel anxiety, depression, or think you may have PTSD, please make an appointment with your doctor and share your concerns. There is help available. Don't wait; make that call today!